The View
from the Top of the Mountain
poems after sixty

Edited by Tom Koontz and Thom Tammaro

First Edition

ISBN: 0-935306-12-9
Library of Congress Catalog Card Number: 81-65930

The Barnwood Press Cooperative
R.R. 2 Box 11C
Daleville, IN 47334

Printed in The United States of America.

Grateful acknowledgment is made for permission to reprint the following:

James Broughton: "Going Through Customs," and "Questions of Farewell" are reprinted from *Odes for Odd Occasions*, ManRoot Press, 1977. "Son of the Godbody" is reprinted from *Song of the Godbody*, ManRoot Press, 1978.

LoVerne Brown: "Safeway Strike," copyright ©1979 LoVerne Brown.

Elmira Bussey: "Beyond Endurance" is reprinted from *Among The Missing*.

Olga Cabral: "Poem About Death" is reprinted from *Darkeness in My Pocket*, Gallimaufry Press, 1976. "Lillian's Chair" and "Picasso's Women" are reprinted from *Occupied Country*, New Rivers Press, 1976. "In The Empire of Ice," "Ladder," and "Night Flight" are reprinted from *In The Empire of Ice*, West End Press, 1980. "Bridges" first appeared in *Milkweed Chronicle*, 1980.

Eleanor Davidson Calenda: "Spinster" first appeared in *The Poet*, Spring 1980.

Elizabeth Eddy: "Riposte to Ben Franklin" first appeared in *Poetry & Magazine*, 1976.

Bela Egyedi: "autumn" first appeared in *Poetry/Windsor/Poesie*.

Ethel Nestell Fortner: "Low Fidelity" first appeared in the *St. Andrews Review*, 1974.

Robert Francis: "Silent Poem," "Blueberries," "Fire Chaconne," and "Light Casualties" are reprinted with permission from *Robert Francis: Collected Poems: 1936-1976*, (University of Massachusetts Press), copyright © 1976 by Robert Francis.

Robert Friend: "The Return" is reprinted from *Somewhere Lower Down*, Menard Press, 1980.

James Hearst: "Lack of Seed Power" first appeared in *Harper's*, 1980. "Responsibility of Being Young" first appeared in *Barnwood*, 1981.

Josephine Jacobsen: "Gentle Reader" and "The Lovers" are reprinted from *The Shade Seller* by Josephine Jacobsen. Copyright ©1968 by *The New Yorker* Magazine, Inc. First appeared in *The New Yorker*. Reprinted by permission of Doubleday & Company, Inc. "Pondicherry Blues" first appeared in *Poetry Now*, 1980.

Joseph Langland: "A Dream Of Love" first appeared in *The Massachusetts Review* and is reprinted from *Any Body's Song*, Doubleday & Company, Inc., 1980.

Howard Nemerov: "The Author to His Body on Their Fifteenth Birthday, 29 ii 80" is reprinted from *Sentences*, by Howard Nemerov. The University of Chicago Press, 1980. Reprinted by permission of the author.

Ann Petry: "A Purely Black Stone" first appeared in *Barnwood*, 1981. "A Purely Black Stone" and "A Real Boss Black Cat" copyright © 1981 Ann Petry.

Carl Rakosi: "Meditation: Melancholy," "Meditation: What is the nature, "Meditation: Psychologist," "Meditation: Lord, what is man?" "Meditation: The old man" first appeared in *Montemora*.

Leonard Wallace Robinson: "In The Whale" first appeared in *The New Yorker*. Reprinted by permission: © 1980 The New Yorker Magazine, Inc. "Squalor and Early Sorrow" first appeared in *New Letters*.

Francis Coleman Rosenberger: "Are You Just Back For A Visit Or Are You Here To Stay?" first appeared in *Poetry*, copyright © 1980 Modern Poetry Association.

Robert Sargeant: "A Woman from Memphis" is reprinted from *A Woman from Memphis*, The Word Works, 1979.

William Stafford: "Absences" first appeared in *Field*, 1979. "Glimpses" first appeared in *American Poetry Review*, 1979. "Waiting in Line" first appeared in *Barnwood*, 1980. "Our Story," "A Story That Could Be True," copyright © 1976 by William Stafford, "Whispered Into The Ground," "Sitting Up Late," copyright © 1974 by William Stafford, "Another Old Guitar," copyright © 1977 by William Stafford, and "Ask Me," copyright © 1975 by William Stafford, are reprinted from *Stories That Could Be True*, 1977, by William Stafford, by permission of Harper & Row, Publishers, Inc.

Adrien Stoutenburg: "Lures" first appeared in *Barnwood, 1981* "Fact Versus Fancy, & Vice Versa" first appeared in *Kayak*.

Peter Viereck: "60th Birthday" is reprinted from *New and Selected Poems*, University Microfilms International (Ann Arbor, MI). "I Have Been Spontaneous in Bermuda" will appear in the collection of new poems, *Applewood*.

Po Chü-i: "A Dream of Mountaineering," "On Being Sixty" are reprinted from *Translations from The Chinese* by Arthur Waley, Alfred A. Knopf, Inc., 1922.

Cover: *Landscape*, ink and wash on paper, by Shokei, courtesy of Nezu Art Museum, Tokyo. Graphics by Barabara LaRue King.

The Barnwood Press Cooperative, a nonprofit, tax-exempt organization for the support of contemporary poetry, reserves only the non-exclusive right, transferred to it by the authors of the poems in *The View from The Top of The Mountain*, to publish those poems in the first and subsequent editions of this anthology.

This book has been published with the support of The Indiana Arts Commission and The National Endownment for The Arts.

Contents

Introduction

Each poem in *The View from The Top of The Mountain* was written after its author had passed the age of fifty-nine. The Barnwood Press Cooperative collected these poems because of our belief that the perspective that results from sixty or more years of observation and contemplation of life is a special one that should be shared and honored. We publish this book in a spirit of celebration of the poetic achievement of a true dream—in the words of Po Chü-i, "a dream of mountaineering," a dream of life.

Readers of this anthology will find interests and attitudes that are held in common by many of the authors, but they will also find a wide range of subjects and of individual sensibilities and styles. The editors did not specify subjects or forms. In our call for submissions, we explained, furthermore, that "the age of the author need not be apparent in the text of the poem, nor need the poem's persona or characters be of any particular age." With a few exceptions in which the authors invited the editors to select from published books of recent work, the poems herein simply present the authors' selections of their work for inclusion in an anthology with our announced perspective.

Many more poems could have appeared in this collection (had there been room), on the grounds of genuineness and significance of experience reported and of emotion expressed. Our primary criterion for acceptance for publication, however, was artistic excellence, judged in accordance with our knowledge of past and present achievements in the art. It is understandable, therefore, that most of the poets whose work has been included are professional writers who have perfected their art over a career of more than forty years. But some of the authors are semi-pros, and some are amateurs. A few writers in the latter groups have only recently begun writing or have returned to the art after having been away for a time raising children or pursuing careers.

The editors wish to express their gratitude for the support received from the members of The Barnwood Press Cooperative and from many poets (including many whose poems were returned). Especially we thank A.E. Claeyssens and Norma G. Maness, for their early encouragement and assistance.

Tom Koontz
Thom Tammaro

To Dorothy Hamilton
writer, teacher, friend

A Dream of Mountaineering

(Written when he was over seventy)

At night, in my dream, I stoutly climbed a mountain,
Going out alone with my staff of holly-wood.
A thousand crags, a hundred hundred valleys—
In my dream-journey none were unexplored
And all the while my feet never grew tired
And my step was as strong as in my young days.
Can it be that when the mind travels backward
The body also returns to its old state?
And can it be, as between body and soul,
That the body may languish, while the soul is still strong?
Soul and body—both are vanities:
Dreaming and waking—both alike unreal.
In the day my feet are palsied and tottering;
In the night my steps go striding over the hills.
As day and night are divided in equal parts—
Between the two, I get as much as I lose.

Po Chü-i
tr. Arthur Waley

On Being Sixty

Addressed to Liu Meng-te, who had asked for a poem.
He was the same age as Po Chü-i.

Between thirty and forty, one is distracted by the Five Lusts;
Between seventy and eighty, one is a prey to
    a hundred diseases.
But from fifty to sixty one is free from all ills;
Calm and still—the heart enjoys rest.
I have put behind me Love and Greed; I have done with
    Profit and Fame;
I am still short of illness and decay and far from decrepit age.
Strength of limb I still possess to seek the rivers and hills;
Still my heart has spirit enough to listen to flutes and strings.
At leisure I open new wine and taste several cups;
Drunken I recall old poems and sing a whole volume.
Meng-te has asked for a poem and herewith I exhort him
Not to complain of three-score, "the time of obedient ears".*

Po Chü-i
tr. Arthur Waley

*Confucius said that it was not till sixty
that "his ears obeyed him".

FROM *SONNETS TO ORPHEUS*

XII

Will transformation! Long for, oh *yearn* for the
    flame,
in which something escapes you, adorned in the changes
    it vaunts.
That Spirit designing, all-planning, which gives earth
    its frame,
loves nothing so much in the upward swing as the
    turning point.

That which is closed up in sameness is already
    hardened.
Shielded, it thinks itself safe in the inconspicuous
    gray?
Wait, something hardest gives warning from afar to the
    hardness.
Beware! An absent hammer is raised.

Whoever pours himself forth as if from a fountain
is known to Knowledge. She leads him delighted through
    cheerful creation,
which often ends at the start and begins with the end.

Each happy space that they pass through astounded
is child or grandchild of separation. And Daphne
    transformed
into laurel feels berries grow, and wants you to change
    yourself into wind.

By Rainer Maria Rilke
tr. by Martha Bartlett

1

THE CRYSTAL SET

A wire sings!
I hear it in my fingertips,
as when sound was first captured
in that dime-size crystal, long ago.

Tirelessly
I would scratch with the fine wire over the dull surface,
feel the bumps and hollows
in my earphoned head thudding.

Touched by the wire
a laughing half-note might disappear
into the darkness of my ears.
My moonface sighed in lost expectancy.
Then suddenly
the waves from a deepthroated organ
rolled over me.

Martha Bartlett

FROM: *MASSES OF HEAD PAIN*
take 25.

what is beauty
when you risk
your wrists
each day
better to pant
or pretend a grunt

at last edgar
wearing a dreary coat
calls on maggie

she in wrap
hardly knows where
the walking is
screams jam
& i got a taste
of you

Guy Beining

3

take 26.

he carries her out
but she carries him in

he wants her legs
of knowledge
more appetite than
a sunday poem
pearl breath streams out
the hours in rows
stack up their expressions

voices travel out
destroyed by feel
a cake of soap in
the bathroom
edgar sees hard polish
& silver years
grandparents to slip
from wash basin

Guy Beining

4

take 27.

to blink &
pretend again

this/this seamy
stringy lady
ink running the mind
had dark birds of wisdom
in her hair
& in an empty chair
the ravens slept

he now soaked in coma
mumbles of debris
& her root
& her whistle
the pulse of lobsters
along his hands

Guy Beining

WAVE PLOTS IN SPACE AND TIME

1

Two loves have brought me to a cold March shore:
The old of ocean and another new:
Gray eyes paired on the breaking gray;
Lips as changeful as the sea.

Tell those who love you, when they look at you,
To leave possession; for your face will shift
With banished Eve from smiling into grief.

Like sandpipers, up and down with the wash,
I follow the wave-play of those lips.

2

From the windowed house Atlantic day.
Renews, you with me, flower-gowned.
After thirty years to watch the dawn rose
Throw petals on the waves. We have no better
Teachers than the gods: ocean, sun
Squander tides of unconditioned love.

For kind, who cares—and who cares not?

3

Grass stems mark the turn of day
By the shadows' conjugate curves;
Wave-concaves, toward noon, focus sun.
Small ones, down the beach, crack musket fire;
The thunder of the great, carried higher,
Thins to a whisper as the surf shoals in.

On the strand of now time's motion rides:
Wind in the grass over migrant dunes,
Sand-ripples shadowed from the low sun.

The most ephemeral most of all endures.

4

Motorbikes barrel the strand. Oil slicks;
Surf brown; sludged foam. Washed no more
In the limitless, illimitable blue.
To float a dream
Of lawns and houses down the Main Line
We slag earth's ocean to a dying pool.
Good times end it sooner; give us good times.

To ride the love-surge of your youth
I could almost pioneer another westward death.

5

The finite effluent takes the sky.
Change rounds on itself, the lift and lean
Crashing always to the shoreward spill,
Restless as the molecular sliding fives
By which (some say) the fluid state obtains.

We ride face backward on the time train.
Hours and miles of distance clacking to more,
Every paired Bosch bubble turns to dream,
Whether of earth or woman.

                                    Cry the other
Sea: spermatic tongues of flame, wider
Than the lost, more changeable—unchanged.

Charles G. Bell

Author's Note: This poem is from an unpublished
book—wave sequences which move recurrently through five
archetypal states of love: LOVE simple; love narrowed, as
in LUST; attached to things (EARTH); perturbed or revers-
ed (WASTE); transcended (SOUL).

SELF-PORTRAIT I: 1979

I watch myself walking towards me:
scrunched up, buttoned, hatted over my ears.
Although it's not that cold,
my old bones want, need warmth, more warmth.
I lean to one side, swaying,
on account of enigmatic pains
which I've decided to accept on faith.
I bet you're thinking,
Poor old lady, she's on her last leg!
That may be, young man,
but when I get home
I'll be rushing for a pen
to get down a certain poem and
maybe take a swish to two
at a Sumi-E painting.
NOW, don't start envying me!

Etta Blum

SELF-PORTRAIT II: 1979

Passing the mirror
in the Ladies' Room,
you stop to stare,
seeing bleak image
of old age.
You are triumphant.
It's not only
the hair's utter
gray, but the way
if falls straightly
to infant softness.
The wrinkles etched clearly.
Dimmed, the
eyes question still,
as always.
At last you understand:
the face is
what it had to grow
into. You approve.

Etta Blum

9

POEM IN AUGUST

No birthday in October
no sing-song & shimmer of nature
I am nearly twice thirty
my blooming years have come & gone.
I am cast in the hot August sun
a golden lion growls from my heart
& loins, I fill his mouth with mine
taste is rank, I do not care—
passion ruts on the ground,
an old woman refusing her role
who sleeps with a double-headed
monster between her legs
unfolding from her guts—
a lion riding her back.
Who will have me at 59
One, who calls himself Husband,
marks time.

Pearl Bond

DAYSTAR EXPRESS
Written on by 65th birthday, 10 November 1978

I am an old youngster who gets up with Venus
I am an old childhood of the dawn
 I worship the morning star
 I ride the morning star
I arise early to run after my downfall

I am an old boy glowing as the light fades
I have a new childhood ready for the dusk
 I dropkick the sunrise
 I polevault to sundown
I perish nightly on my nonstop dayshift

James Broughton

11

QUESTIONS OF FAREWELL
A Letter to Lama Govinda

Before I step off this old turnabout
    this tinkly surround
    with wounds abounding
tell me, what pulls the heart around it
and bears the wisdom out?

Before I must practice my exit march
    from this circus ground
    this circular round
tell me, what tempo comes out of time
to set the whole medley on its ear?

Before any elegies drown out my song
    and all that resounds
    has come unwound
tell me, if you know, what major key
winds up the soul's music box?

James Broughton

SONG OF THE GODBODY

I breathe you I contain you I propel you
I am your opening and closing
I am your rising and falling
I am your thrust and surrender

I stiffen you I melt you I energize
I quicken your humor and heartache
I set the spark to your fluid
I stir your mixable blessing

I am your inside operator
I stretch I sweat I maneuver
I flex your will and your man power
I polish your launching pad

I prime your engines of quest
I fan your spontaneous combustion
I drive your vehicle of dreams
I accelerate your valor and risk

I am at the root of your folly
I am at the top of your form
In you I caper and flourish
In you I become what I am

You are my cheerful vicissitude
You are my sturdy weakness
I am your faithful bedfellow
I am your tenacious secret

I connect your links
I replenish your seeds
I bathe in your bloodstream
I bask in the raw of your nature

I am the conductor of pulse and impulse
I am the director of anatomical play
You are my theater of nervous charades
You are my circus of knack and bungle

13

I am your unheeded prompter
I am the slips of your tongue
I am the catch in whatever you think
I am the quirk in what you are sure of

I carry a lantern through your labyrinth
I call to you from your vitals
You hear me best when you marvel
You hear me least when you whimper

You are my ancient You are my child
You are the brother of all your heroes
My earnest monkey My ticklish lion
You are my zoo and my sanctum

I tune up your instruments
I play on your organs
I strum in your breast
I croon in your head

I elixirate your phallus
I enter your every orifice
I impregnate every beginning
I effervesce I rhapsodize

You plunge into motley waters
You catch on fire when you love
You are my liquid opal
You are my burning bush

I sprout your sperm and your egg
I spawn the engodments of flesh
I shape the new body of Adam
I reshape the old body of Eve

I engender all the women of men
I generate the men of all women
I love you in every man's body
I live you in every man's lover

Trust that I know my own business
Cherish your fact and your fettle
Respect your perpetual motion
Relish your frisky divinity

You are my ripening godling
You are my fidgety angel
You are my immortal shenanigan
You are my eroding monument

I am ever your lifelong bodyguard
I am always your marathon dancer
Let your feet itch with my glory
Dance all the way to your death

James Broughton

GOING THROUGH CUSTOMS
A Bon Voyage for Me

Before our first goodbye let me say a last hello,
let my baggage declaration be an open book.
I enjoy a crooked road but I like a record straight.

I'm nothing very special, in my very special way.
I'm a fish out of water who bathes in the sun
but I try to keep my tides on an even keel.

I figure we're all aboard the same lifesize boat.
Naked we shall sink, as we first came ashore.
But I chuckle too much to get seasick about it.

I like acrobats, wine, birdsong and puzzles,
I like church bells, picnics and hot steam baths,
I like my nights out and I like them tucked in bed.

My dreams are more real than the fact of my sleeping
but I always go to bed with my suitcase packed.
Be it earthquake or elopement, I want to be ready.

Like Lucifer a bit, I'm busy loitering about,
one eye on the ball and one on the goalkeeper.
I'm a lazy ball of fire, catch me if you can.

You won't catch commonsense sticking round me.
I hate things common and I never was sensible,
I post urgent letters in the trunks of trees.

My penpals are unlettered demons and saints.
I deal in romancement, I ecstasize man.
Love is my warrior to slay the Giant Sloth.

My particular sidekicks are Pan and Jesus
who are working out a world-wind pas-de-deux.
We often sit laughing by old Lao-Tzu's river.

My true-born parents are Hermes and Aphrodite
who gave me a new life where both ends meet.
All I have to declare is the jewel in my lotus.

So I'm a happy medium, a golden meanie,
whose pivot may wobble but who's still on his toes.
A fool and his rapture are not easily parted.

Don't take me at my word if you have a wiser.
Life's not a neat fit, it comes in all sizes.
Wear out your own passport, wave when you're drowning.
    And so be it a goodbye and bye.

                        James Broughton

SAFEWAY STRIKE

I won't go to the supermarket today.
I never cross picket lines,
even when the issue's absurd,
as this one may be—
having in the lean thirties
stood often in lines that could not hold;
remembering the shockwaves of hate
that swept like an ice-bearing window
to chill the marrow of bone;
when hunched miners,
coughing and blinking,
were flattened with clubs
by the hired mercenaries from Seattle;
pink blood frothed from the head
of Gus Aronson
before he fell,
and the wife of the mayor,
coming out of the tavern,
spat her whiskeyed saliva
in that broken dead face. . . .

But there was love, too,
caught in those wavering lines,
a liferope of caring
that dragged us upward
out of those meagre days;
it is for the love of comrades,
folded in memory like a flattened clover,
it is for Al and Margaret
that I do not go to the Safeway.

LoVerne Brown

18

PLEASED TO MEET YOU

"oh my god," she said, *"Jean Don Carlo!*
he doesn't have to speak *English!*
he has *everything!*
mainly, it's his *eyes!"*

"ah, bullshit," you said.

"no," she said, "he's devastatingly charming,
even *you* would like him!"

it was only a night's conversation
only a bit of a night's conversation
and a year elapsed. . . .

then one night you walked into a small party
with her
and there were various introductions
and then she said,
"and this is Jean Don Carlo!"

hello.
hello.

pleased.
pleased.

you shake hands.

Jean Don Carlo
had almost no chin
almost no eyes
no charm
nothing.

even when he sits down
it is like nothing
sitting down.

the night brings nothing new
to change him
although he now speaks
some English.

he makes his living selling French
racing bikes in America.

there are other people about and there
is nothing else to do but drink. . . .

on the drive back in
you say nothing to her about Jean Don Carlo
and she says nothing to you
about Jean Don Carlo
and that's very good
except that you wonder about all the other things
she has told you
and then you let that go too
because nothing has been very accurate anyhow
in the city in the nation in the
newspapers in the universe. . . .

next time it will be something else she'll say
about a new rock group or a new vitamin
or a way to suspend yourself in steam
in the casket-like contraption
for only $15 an hour
you are not touched by
atmospheric pressures.

it's ALWAYS been Jean Don Carloes
with their pants down and
nothing to show.

shake hands with this poem.

Charles Bukowski

PICK—6

the little old men:
what happened?

I see them at the
track.

this one
takes tiny little steps
3 inches at a time
in old striped pants.

another
not so little
but old—
he looks like a
pregnancy
it all hangs down
over his belt
and he ignores it
although
it must be
⅓ of his body.

another is a
dwarf.
he is followed by
a prostitute who
keeps screaming at him,
"hey, Johnny, where the hell
you going?"
but Johnny keeps
walking in circles like
a wound-up toy
and he has this
large head and
it's more beautiful
than anything
I've seen in the
movies or
anywhere.

I look about and
there are all these
aged and misshapen men
everywhere
walking about
talking
drinking coffee and beer
smoking. . . .

there are
hundreds of them
but nobody notices
or if they do
they are gently
polite about it.

they are
all about.
some have no
arms.
others
no eyes
no legs
no feet.
one has no
mouth
it's sucked in
dry like a
cat's bunghole.

they come to the
racetrack
every day
and I am
there too.
there aren't so
many women.
I don't know
where
the women go.

then
the dwarf comes
spinning by
his arms whirling
rapidly
he gives me a
good knock on
the knee
almost
flooring me.
"hey, Johnny," says
the prostitute, "where
the hell you going?"

people think that
all they have
at the racetracks
are horses. it's
not true. that's
why I come home
so tired
every night.

Charles Bukowski

BEYOND ENDURANCE

I can take piled-up snow drifts that attend to their own removal. I can take the need for rubber boots, impassable crossings, slippery sidewalks. I can take Nor'easters knocking on the window panes. I can take all these, though at times I have felt like the horse must have felt that was given a diet of sawdust, and died after he got used to it. I cannot take the spring. I cannot take the beneficial loan of soft, southern air. I cannot take crocuses, snowdrops, tulips, daffodils, anything that has the spunkiness to work itself upward through the ground. I cannot take a deluge of forsythia against gray houses— it makes them too beautiful. I cannot take magnolia trees on Commonwealth Avenue, or any other place. I cannot take the bewildering appearance of the pink cherry tree down the street, and the queen for a day on the back lawn—the old pear tree. I cannot take the first early morning song of a robin. I cannot take wanting to cry like a baby. I cannot take the elements at work changing human stones into unhardened gelatine. I cannot take being overwhelmed by creation. I cannot take the spring.

Elmira Bussey

PICASSO'S WOMEN

In Cagliostro's mirror the magician keeps all his women:

the green woman with plants for fingers
the woman of snowstorms; calm flakes fall from her eyelids
the woman who leans on her arm; it becomes bread on the table
the woman whose face is a ripe pod just burst open
the woman with the faces of several strangers under one hat
the woman all circular arms; the kiss of her face bends over
the woman whose face grows roots like a vegetable
the woman whose head floats off as her shoulders leave the room

women made of fruit women made of machine parts
women's eyes like spiders minerals or medallions
women's eyes with small wheels whirring behind them
women like walking hieroglyphs of women
women like fetishes of rag or of coconut bark
women of fishbone women of cactus
a woman like a watermelon a woman of green rind:
open her face and her rows of black seeds are laughing

The magician has shuffled their features like decks of cards
he wants his women cardboard he wants them Cretan vases
he tosses them noses they catch each other's chins
but no matter how he deals the One-Eyed Woman always turns up
she of the double profile who watches both ways:
the archetypal ancestress changing but changeless

Knowing the ripe peach is a guttering candle
knowing the pitcher is pouring its own clay
knowing the flowers are lamps blowing themselves out
the women watch from Cagliostro's mirror
as the magician slowly turns into a piece of sundried driftwood
under the grave eyes of women forbidden to age.

Olga Cabral

LILLIAN'S CHAIR
(For Lillian Lowenfels)

Lillian has just arisen from her chair.
She has gone into her garden to commune with snails
to answer the birds' questions.
She has left her shawl and her cane
and that iron leg brace.
Won't she need her shawl in the garden?
Won't she be feeling the cold?

And she has forgotten her sling
thrown it carelessly aside,
the crumpled black satin
in which she cradled her dead arm
for seventeen years.
In one hand she took her straw basket
in the other her pruning shears:
"That bush needs seeing to," she muttered
and went looking for red clover, queen anne's lace.

What is she doing so long in the garden?
Where has she gone with her red hair?
She just grew tired of sitting and watching.

A vivid light pulled her into the leaves.
Woolen shawl, satin sling, iron brace—
she just walked out on them all.
Left us this empty chair.

Olga Cabral

POEM ABOUT DEATH

I don't want to die so many small deaths.
The death of somnambulists in all-night cafeterias
or clerks following their steel-file coffins to the grave.
The small funerals of varnishes, job interviews.

I don't want to die the life of AT&T.
The brain bland as gelatin in its brainbox,
a small electrode embedded in its gray crevasses
implanting canned laughter, military commands and jokes stale
                as frenchfries.

Listen! I have lived from Spain to Spain.
I was young in Guernica. I grew old in Santiago.
I tried to stop all the bleeding, to bandage wounds with
                petitions.
I tried to stop the blind bombing capability with my fists
                and cries.

And all the while what deaths! What grandiose harvests of
                corpses!
What chimneys! What soft targets! What magnificent madhouses!
And the death of choices:
death by starving or death by the firing squad.

There are deaths and deaths.
There is the death of Kennecott Copper climbing 7/8ths to
                corporate heaven
as someone is pushed from a helicopter somewhere over Chile
for eating meat instead of garbage for the first time in his life.

You say this is not a subject for a poem?
That it is not even a poem?
That I should leave death to the professionals?
That poetry should be above "all that"?

Listen! There is a wind that slices iron.
The dead keep their accounts. The living grow stronger.
I want to die a little each day living the deaths of the people.
Bleeding because I am alive.

Olga Cabral

27

IN THE EMPIRE OF ICE

In circumpolar night
in bitter drifts
on the black knife-edge of existence
where nothing is wanted
nothing alive
has any right to be
there in the keen raw cut of razored winds
the Emperor of birds
is born

Spectral in frost
the tall bird-forms
planted on broad webbed feet
stand manlike in wide ring
in a wall
a clumsy windbreak between polar whirlwinds
and the bird nurseries

No human eye has seen them
patient as stuffed birds
mate spelling mate
each one in turn
with body heat and fold of blubber
faithful to vigil
to the fragile egg
until its mate returns from icy feeding

Oh call it something:
stupid birds
know only ice worlds
threat of rigor mortis
but if not faith
call it a shielding
a little lamp in the great wind of death.

Olga Cabral

28

LADDER

Oh, here is a ladder standing by itself in the air!
Who has left it lying about?
What careless angel or archetype
of sky goddess?
And what is its purpose if not to climb?
I accept the challenge. I ascend
and everything changes.

I encounter constellations
of unnamed insects
their metallic voices glistening
in the dark
fish gliding silently in the sky
a whole ocean twittering
and the birds
fellow wayfarers asking:
are there forests we have never seen?

Is there an up or down to this journey?
Am I ascending or descending?
What is it I am getting nearer to
as I get farther away?
Down there that little life:
was it mine?
The stars meanwhile are larger, fiercer.

Olga Cabral

NIGHT FLIGHT
(For John Beecher)

In diamond-black darkness
I am flying over the sleeping continent
in the cabin of a lighted jet
where I sit elbow to elbow
a package among packages
in a cargo of tired human flesh.

The lights in the cabin are dimmed
and all sleep but I
cannot
thinking of you friend I have left
thinking you spoke to me through jets of oxygen
a ritual mask of sorts
that did not disguise but has already distanced you
thinking the simple air that we must all breathe
hardly keeps you alive
another hardwon day and another
thinking that we may not meet again
this side of Lethe

Staring out
through the tiny porthole
thinking too of all those I have loved
gone so suddenly
and soon
these three years past
"the tears of things"
dazzle

The moon follows us
a serene death's-head
and pours its cold white calcium
the same millennial light
as long ago over abysmal swamps
where archaeopteryx lifted its crude clawed wing
and tried for the stars

All has led to this
this moment
jet engine burning up time
crossing
the dark roads of the sky
I press my face against the small black oval
and study the maps of darkness spread below
the mysterious charts unreeling

Rafts of medusas
thin patches of palest violet
floating in black liquor
iron and ashen
scars of eternal
snow ridges and snow peaks
a color on the edge of color
color that has no name
lampblack blotters
that soak up all the forests
with here and there a seed of light
a drop of mercury
shining
then the industrial
jewels the swords necklaces tiaras and loops of light
the sleeping metropolises

And trailing low on the horizon
that great star-tracing
the Dipper
so near I might reach out across the world
and grasp the glittering handle:
fiery design
of geometrically pure and perfect
Cup of heaven
that tilts and spills
its draught of darkness

Companions of the dream
radiant company
did you not drink
deeply and well
all that was offered?

And I go on
and will return
to the tables of our feasting
pick up the empty cups
the glasses stained with joy
and place my lips upon the place
your breath still clouds.

Olga Cabral

BRIDGES

This bridge
which has neither arch nor span nor pillar
this bridge
which is not of wood or stone or metal
this bridge
which crosses no land or water or air
yet stands
indestructible over the swift black torrents of forgetting
over the rushing debris of centuries
over the collapse of countless dynasties and kingdoms

This bridge
which is made of the frailest of whispers
the sound of a writing-brush moving swiftly on paper
this bridge of words
is the bridge that crosses over a thousand years
where we meet somewhere in the middle
and you hand me a flower of the plum tree
and I return with your verses
as you go back to your century
and your yellow sleeves disappear in the mists of not-being.

Olga Cabral

SPINSTER

Pearl hair
Undone
By knotted hands.
Pride's crown
Above a sparse skinned face.

Her thin lips part
in a second's sensuous grace.
Then
Her puritan hands
reach up
to plait and pin.

Held in for seventy years
in her own cage,
Hair whispers
above the wrinkles
and the shut purse mouth,
There is a woman
Waiting
in this house.

Eleanor Davidson Calenda

INTERIM for Tom

Unable to stay
death
we fight
ourselves each other
you work at breathing
my words run onto paper
confronting God doctors
what we are will be

From our vacuum
you say, "Remember. . ."
and we are briefly
whole again.

Lillie D. Chaffin

RIPOSTE TO BEN FRANKLIN

"Seek out the older women
they will be experienced
and they will be
grateful."
Well, sonny, or old man, or
whatever you turn out to be,
whether i am frigid sub-
tropical tropical temperate
satisfactory or
even grateful,
you are not
going
to
be
tie that to
the tail
of your
kite
and
fly
it

Elizabeth Eddy

JELLYROLL I'M COMING BEAUTIFUL or
EVERYBODY WAIT FOR ME

no flowers
all i ask
is
just a real jazzband play
take the A Train i would now
if i thought it'd get me anywhere
all the One O'Clock Jumps there are
Harry's Two O'Clock
Harvard Blues oh Jimmy Rushing please
Stompin at the Savoy
the Saints naturally after all who
do you think i am and
Bill Bailey Won't You Please Come Home
it's safe to
now

Elizabeth Eddy

OPTIMISM

past-60—the ease!
which lord would
command you to
climb the fuji-san?

NIGHT TRAIN

close your eyes, child:
no more beauty between
this station
and the terminus

AUTUMN

a-shiver
the park-trees
how did they know
my solitude?

bẽla egyedi

ON A CLEAR DAY

Down a long hill in Granada
swinging hands like children in summer
we found a shop in the woods.

I wanted to buy you a dashing hat
wide worked leather to speak of me.

You touched it, tried it on, willing to wear it.
It was expensive and only a hat.

In the town below we laughed
and drank small brandies
talking of other things.

From above the reins tugged
—oh, we had knives to cut them!—
young voices called our true names.

Hatless, out of fashion
we leaned into the pitch of the hill
on the climb back.

Vesle Fenstermaker

THE PATTERN

Sometimes I feel as if I had been set down
in the corner of a pattern
and given a weaving work to do
like an ancient artisan
given a corner of a great tapestry to work upon.
But I can't see the grand design
and so I don't know
if I am weaving well,
perhaps making a beautiful corner
attached to a chaos
of dropped stitches and botched detail
pieced with other good bits,
or whether I am doing the dropping and botching,
indeed whether I am working
with nothing on nothing
alone in a wilderness.
While resting I look over my work
and think about not knowing all the design
and wonder if I should do something else.
But after a time my hands make weaving motions
and I think about the pattern again.
I return to my corner.

Margaret Flanagan

LOW FIDELITY

When the letter
never came and never came
a silence
crisp
insistent
hard-edged
twisted my day threads
until thought drowned
in throbbing stereo sound.

After the day-noise
quiet
folds me in a smooth robe.

Night wires drone
across rooftops and valleys,
over plains to a town
through miles and miles of moonlight.

Under the layers i dream dark.

Ethel Nestell Fortner

SILENT POEM

backroad leafmold stonewall chipmunk
underbrush grapevine woodchuck shadblow

woodsmoke cowbarn honeysuckle woodpile
sawhorse bucksaw outhouse wellsweep

backdoor flagstone bulkhead buttermilk
candlestick ragrug firedog brownbread

hilltop outcrop cowbell buttercup
whetstone thunderstorm pitchfork steeplebush

gristmill millstone cornmeal waterwheel
watercress buckwheat firefly jewelweed

gravestone groundpine windbreak bedrock
weathercock snowfall starlight cockcrow

Robert Francis

LIGHT CASUALTIES

Light things falling—I think of rain,
Sprinkl of rain, a little shower
And later the even lighter snow.

Falling and light—white petal-fall
Apple and pear, and then the leaves.
Nothing is lighter than a falling leaf.

Did the guns whisper when they spoke
That day? Did death tiptoe his business?
And afterwards in another world

Did mourners put on light mourning,
Casual as rain, as snow, as leaves?
Did a few tears fall?

Robert Francis

BLUEBERRIES

faint blue dark blue their bloom
untarnished wild rose ferns
the hayscented brushing a granite boulder

blueberries highbush lowbush
and silence old-fashioned silence
a single towee "drink your teee"

white clouds sky pasture blueberries
a bird's booty a boy's occupation
stain of blueberry on a boy's mouth

and all around the blueberry-colored
hills dark blue faint blue blue
beyond blue the farther the fainter

silence except once and again
an invisible valley train like a
lost calf bawling-calling its mother

is it Butter Hill or the northern Kearsarge
or the little hills of Concord and Henry
fresh out of jail sun standing still

Sunday morning gleam of white steeple
bell unheard oh nothing heard at all
save solitary soliloquizing cricket

sweetfern John Greenleaf and juniper
the blueberry-pickers lost to one another
"the August day ablaze on lonely hills"

Robert Francis

FIRE CHACONNE

1

Flare of match
Cupped hands its vestal temple.

2

Firefly, your green
Spark on the green darkness.

3

I burn
Therefore I am.

4

Single in window
Candle, what are you saying?

5

What fate?
Wind or your own down-burning?

6

The cold stars
Their incredible heat.

7

Blue juniper
Berry: two summers' sun.

8

Con fuoco
You violins, your incandescence.

9

Flaming in fall
Gorgeous the poison ivy.

10

"Scotland's burning.
Pour on water." No, no, not Scotland.

11

Ambivalent fire
Our love, our life, our fear.

12

Scarlet the night sky.
Bonfire, beacon, holocaust?

13

"God is love.
Reader, flee from the wrath to come."

14

Savonarola
The stones of Florence still weeping.

15

Fire lizard?
How far the moist woodland salamander!

16

The salt sea
Dyes the driftwood hearth.

17

True poem
Burns with undiminishing fuel.

18

Bonfire on snow
Twice beautiful: symbol and fact.

19

Almighty sun
Father of all our fires.

20

Fire opal
As if all gems were flashing.

Robert Francis

TO HIS IMPUDENCE ON HIS COMING IMPOTENCE

Well, well, Sir Bone-Head,
you who have had so many ups and downs,
you'll be getting your come-uppance soon,
you won't be able to keep it up much longer.
You who never needed to understand
so long as you could stand,
can you understand
the simple long and short of it?
It won't be long, Simpleton,
before it will be "So long!"

Soon you will retire—
permanently.
You who never could or never would
discriminate
will not disgrace me any more,
you, who no matter who invited you,
were always glad to come.

Take a well-earned rest,
Muscle-man.
Shrink back into yourself,
turn shrinking violet,
and try to enjoy yourself
in your retirement.
Tell yourself stories—
all cock and ball,
and lumpishly boast, you lump,
of all your holes-in-one.

To think you were, my Lord Senility,
my chief divinity,
my three-in-one:
Father, Son, and Holy Ghost.
Now wholly Ghost.

A fallen potentate,
but potent still
to haunt me.

Robert Friend

48

THE RETURN

Endlessly endlessly
eyes washed clear of memory
eyes washed clear of pain

they return
to where the unborn wait their turn
to the kingdom of no history

at last at last.

But the memory of the mystery
lives in the idiot tongue
that drivels helplessly

Do not be born! Do not be born!
to those who will not hear
but throng the burning gate

impatiently impatiently.

Robert Friend

BYE-BYE, BESSIE

Bessie's leaving the Home.
She had to, or become
on of them.

No longer will she sit
rocking little Mitzi,
a sweet baby of ninety-four.

Nor will nonagenarian, Bill,
talking to himself
in a Mr. Magoo voice,

be able to come up,
suddenly, behind Bessie,
grab a feel, and make
her blush.

She won't have to
constantly coax poor Tom,
who smells like an inmate
of a stockyard, to take
a bath.

No more waving goodby
to Millie, anxious to get home
"to cook dinner" for a family
long grown, and gone.

Bessie will rock in her trailer
trying to keep her hands
busy.

Bobbie Goldman

RESPONSIBILITY OF BEING YOUNG

All I knew concerned my
errand and I felt proud
to be entrusted with that.
My breathless haste prompted
bare legs and feet. Father
needed Andrew to help with
the work, and I knocked at
his mother's door. The woman
who opened it had long sad eyes.
"He can't come," she explained,
"he drownded Sunday, they was
all swimming and he drownded."
Her words flew over my head,
their sense out of my reach.
"But Papa wants him," I insisted,
"to help with the work."
"He drownded yesterday," she said
and gently closed the door.
I stood outside, hands full
of my unfinished errand, wondering
if Father would be cross with me.

James Hearst

LACK OF SEED POWER

He drooped like a wilted flower
this bright bay stallion too weak
in his flesh to breed the mare
who stood dripping in her heat.
He walked around her, nosed her
and hung his head. My Grandfather
said, "Too many trips to the well."
but I scorned the argument, I wanted
the stallion to rise on his hind feet,
grip the mare with forelegs and teeth,
and squeeze into her with strokes
of his muscled rump. I felt
shamed by his failure, this insult to
potency. Beyond the yard I ran to
a clover field where bobolinks
nested and the child in me asked
the future man, how many chances
have we missed, even for stars,
seeds we lack that might have grown
into marvels we never dreamed of?

James Hearst

LATE PORTRAITS OF THE BARD

I

Never very casual
I wore tomorrow's shoes,
faking there were no yesterdays.
I lived on air and apricots.
If I wished it was summer always.
I wore no hat,
the wind was grateful.
When tornados came
I turned up my collar.
The world yammered death calls
turning over like a seal
day after day.
Yesterday I dried my eyes.
Did the world die?
Are there no more zoos?

II

Never late or early
they arrive
almost by appointment.

I'm not alone.
I'm not with someone else.

It's the visiting hour
and in they come,
not to disappoint me.

III

If they thought me
they wouldn't know me.
It wouldn't be me.
If it were me
they couldn't think me.
They'd have to rethink me.
If they rethought me
it would only be me
finished thinking of me.
If they couldn't know me
and couldn't rethink me
you reading me
come much closer to me.

IV

Tonight something different
for a change: someone
friendly to sit next to.
—Will you let me?

Then patiently—Of course.
—But you don't have to,
it's just a whim, you know.
—I know, but I like whims.

—I'd like to creep
into your mouth, go through
your nose, your toenails,
tear out your privates,
come back and empty
your face to those
big brown eyes that turn
on the women. You'll let me?

—Yes, if you promise one thing.
—Anything at all.
—Promise when you're done
you'll never leave me.

V

—With all women the wanting,
with some the naked soul,
with others the handout
from a beggar's bowl.
From some women a touch-me
tit, from some a jeer,
from others the glad hand
of the conventioneer.

Balked by women to the end,
his laid bones jarred
to every ghoul's tread
in the open graveyard.

VI

Delete the lying passage,
cut off the hand that wrote it.
Is it yours or is it yours?
No matter—plenty of us here
are dying to move in.
Whistle, someone's sure to come,
pen in hand, panting to begin.
Go ahead and do it.
You're rich, you beggar.
You've got a clean page
to start with.

Edwin Honig

THE TRIUMPH OF LOVE

As from some grand
Venetian ballroom ceiling
Veronese's cupids
Gaze
Down, ringed
About the cupola,
Coronas of bright hair
Encircling them with light, suspended
There, clipped sturdy wings
Folded, chin in hand
Or holding tight the attic balcony which like
The top rung of a ladder wells
Dizzily above us who look up,
Heads thrown back, craning, seeking our
Reflected stare:

So toward the sleeping child do we
Converge,
Eyelids lowered and look down,
Once more so moved that all
Space dwindles
And the Palace walls
Are scaled to inches by our deepening love.

Barbara Howes

EARLY SUPPER

Laughter of children brings
    The kitchen down with laughter.
While the old kettle sings
Laughter of children brings
To a boil all savory things.
    Higher than beam or rafter,
Laughter of children brings
    The kitchen down with laughter.

So ends an autumn day,
    Light ripples on the ceiling,
Dishes are stacked away;
So ends an autumn day.
The children jog and sway
    In comic dances wheeling.
So ends an autumn day,
    Light ripples on the ceiling.

They trail upstairs to bed,
    And night is a dark tower.
The kettle calls; instead
They trail upstairs to bed,
Leaving warmth, the coppery-red
    Mood of their carnival hour.
They trail upstairs to bed,
    And night is a dark tower.

                        Barbara Howes

MERCEDES

Hopscotch
    Through patches
    Of light, a greeneyed
Dominican slanted
    From palm-frond street-shadow in
To a job, to stay on, to be safer;
But by June, daubed soap on her mirror:
Mercedes de la Rosa esta muerta

Mercedes had
    Work Casuarina—long days:
    "San Francisco, San Francis-
    Co, San Fran. . ." written fifty-three
    Times. . . "In my grandmother's garden
Tomatoes grew, red whole
Hearts, we ate them; they said
    'Mercedes de la Rosa is dead' "

Dream-knives
    Cut out dolls—but I'll
    Help them—that leaf,
    Falling, is a dory. . .
Men: their pants
Pressed to the coil of a whip,
    Shoot billiard
    Eyes at me. . .
Merced es de la Rosa

I can hide my dolls, my
    Cuckoo-clock, though his beak
    Orders me to dance;
Sequins, I glue gold pieces, I sew
Justice on chiffon,
All colors—as I whirl,
    They dance—how my body aches!
    I must nail my cuckoo. . .The
Spinning mirror splinter:
    Mercy befits the Rose

Next day, duck with two heads,
Her radio quacked to itself; a needle
Slanted through the cuckoo's
    Heart; lint of chiffon
Rocked in Erzulie's breeze. . . "People
    Do strange sometimes," she had said,
    And,
Mercedes de la Rosa is dead

                                    Barbara Howes

PONDICHERRY BLUES
(for voice and snare-drum)

Mrs. Pondicherry was/ fat and mean,
she had four/ pug/ dogs and a limousine
black/ as West Virginia coal;
and she troubled herself about her soul,
yes, she surely was concerned/ about her soul.

Father O'Hare was thin as a steeple,
the poor and the lonely were his passion and his people.
Pondicherry would ask/ that man to come to dinner
and talk/ to him/ about the Sinner.
And Father O'Hare got very/ very/ tired of Mrs. Pondicherry,
he got/ raw-bone/ tired of Pondicherry.

She changed her will like/ she changed her furs
cause she surely did know that they both were hers,
and she drove that man beside himself
with her wills/ and her pelts/ and her pugs/ and her pelf,
she drove him purely beside himself.

One day she was sitting on her velvet seat
her mink/ round her shoulders and her footstool for her feet
and a cushion for/ each/ pug;
her heart gave a leap and she fell on the rug,
she fell/ right/ down/ on her big/ red/ rug.

They put her into/ bed and called Father O'Hare
but he couldn't get there and he couldn't get there
and she lay on her bed for a/ solid/ hour
and she didn't say a word cause she didn't own the power,
didn't own the power to say/ a single word.

Her mind was thin and cold as a hag,
in her eyes was a beggar with a/ bowl/ and a/ rag,
and her ears/ heard/ a cold/ wind start
to blow the trash round the alleys of her heart,
to blow/ cold/ trash round the gutters of the heart.

But Father O'Hare he was/ serving the poor,
he never reached the house and he never crossed the door
till she closed her eyes and/ she stopped her breath
in the lonesome/ slum/ of death
that dark/ trashy/ street of/ death.

Josephine Jacobsen

THE LOVERS

The lovers lie in the shelter of night, the lovers
lie in each other's arms in night's crux:
the clock stopped and stars still and fire
unlit, in each other's arms lie the lovers.

Still clock and stopped stars are not true:
cold dust blows from the stars, cold iron roars
through space, time ticks trapped in the two
lovers' wrists. False, stopped clock and still stars.

On the cold hearth, to kindle the lovers' fire,
stuffed under logs lie inly rage and retribution;
on a nail on the wall, stretched arms and folded feet
hang and motionlessly reproduce an execution.

Here the stars make no sound, there is no wind, no clock.
Once an animal cried out in the tall cold meadow
grass, beyond the glass cried out, addressing owl or fox.
Who will stay the lovers in their single shadow?

The lovers lie in the shelter of their deaths;
though they move, now, to part, it is a feint at most:
who were two have died, and are safe in a single breath:
they are discovered, found with all the lost.

Josephine Jacobsen

61

GENTLE READER

Late in the night when I should be asleep
under the city stars in a small room
I read a poet. A poet: not
a versifier. Not a hot-shot
ethic-monger, laying about
him; not a diary of lying
about in cruel cruel beds, crying.
A poet, dangerous and steep.

O God, it peels me, juices me like a press;
this poetry drinks me, eats me, gut and marrow
until I exist in its jester's sorrow,
until my juices feed a savage sight
that runs along the lines, bright
as beasts' eyes. The rubble splays to dust:
city, book, bed, leaving my ear's lust
saying like Molly, yes, yes, yes O yes.

Josephine Jacobsen

A DREAM OF LOVE

Once upon a time
three brothers kept three horses
in a farmyard near a forest not far from a magnificent castle.
According to the old story,
one was black, one brown, and one white.
Each night one of the brothers caught his own horse in the
    early evening,
and in the glimmering darkness
he tried to ride it up a great glass hill
into that fairy kingdom.

And somewhwere three beautiful horses,
with stars just under their forelocks
and hooves aglow in the moonlight,
nicker out of my childhood
and neigh in the distant meadows.
They stand at night in the pastures
with Bell and King and Beauty,
with Czar and Kate by the river
munching the grass by the timber
in the hills of northeastern Iowa,
wild in the harness of spingtime,
tame in the woodland of summer;
with May and June, gray-dappled,
mild in their stalls in the winter,
trotting with sleighs and wagons,
straining at tugs in the snowdrifts,
farting out loud in the village,
working and sweating and sleeping;
with Roxy and Trixy and Mable,
biting and pawing and snorting
when led to the western stallion,
ears flat on their foreheads, breeding,
their nostrils flaring, kicking,
till their hind legs set like pillars;
with Daisy and Bill and Lady
chucking for oats in the morning,
chortling for hay in the evening,
and at county fairs with sulkeys
racing the silver jockeys
and galloping over the hillsides.

My hands still fiddle with those bridles still,
the steel bits sliding over the white shining teeth,
past the dark elastic lips and pink tongues
swallowing into their soft throats.
I pull the reins taut; my arms tighten on their sleek muscles,
and again the polished hooves go clattering
out of the moonlit barnyard and on to the glass hill
where the breathless lady waits with her gossamer gowns and
    pale lips, chill as the night,
for the breath of her one true lover.
Daisy and Lady and Beauty,
we curry your hair in the morning,
your manes in the morning combing,
braiding your tails in the morning,
your velvet nostrils rubbing,
your rumps all silken, slapping;
on your barrel backs still climbing
I bury my face in your manes.
I snuggle my crotch on your withers,
my legs on your rib-flanks wrapping
to touch my feet to your belly.
And we walk and trot and gallop
out of the barns to the roadway
and up the road to the mailbox
and over the hills to the neighbors,
then back again to the barnyard
where I clean your stalls of manure
and bed you down for the evening
in bundles of golden straw.

Black Beauty, I think, is still whinnying in the orchards and
    weeping by waterfalls.
Postillions, coaches and schooners are running wild in their old
    tracks.
Flicka has tossed her tail up again west of Cheyenne and is
    headed into the mountains.
Smoky the Cowhorse is languishing in his harness,
trying to make that shriveled heart grow back again to full size.
The Red Pony and spotted horses are asleep in the
    bookshelves,
and Rosa Bonheur has scribbled magnificent horses all
    over the one-room schoolhouse wall.

Horses are standing by roadways,
charging over the sage-brush
in their oiled and studded saddles;
they are swimming the swollen rivers
through Wyoming, leaping and bucking
and plunging the dust-storms of cattle;
Old Paint is off to Montana,
walking the tourists in mountains
and standing by livery stables
and threshing grain on the prairies.

And somewhere in the local theaters of Spring Grove, Minnesota,
    and Decorah, Iowa,
legions of horses are rising and leaping out of the wild
    Atlantic
onto the Brittany beaches.
Their sea-weed manes are rising and falling, their
    hooves
rising and falling, the wind-driven grass rising
and falling over the dunes,
and the dark French rustlers with their stiff black hats
are throwing silver lariats everywhere out of the hills.

And the Good Men are riding their horses,
and the Bad Men riding their horses,
the stage coach is whipping its horses,
and the Indians are riding their horses,
and the Tartars are riding their horses,
and Ghenghis Khan and the Chinese
emperors riding their horses.
And horses are guarding the palace,
and Lawrence is riding his horses
with all his Arabians running
to the muffled drums of the sand.

And the great blue horses of Franz Marc
stand in Bavaria near Benedicktbeuren with their strict
    geometric rumps,
and Dutch horses wait near courtyards fat as burghers.
By the hay wains set by streams, horses are no more than a
    mound or a lamp-post.

And where is that young blue Spanish boy with his elegant
   mare?
Are they dreaming of blankets of flowers
falling over the pastel horses charging through steeple-chases
   out of the suburbs of Paris?
Or the cavalry milling by Moscow, the horses like dreary
   plains?
Or horses like trumpets and bugles falling, blood-stained, out
   of the sky?

There are princes arriving on chargers
and departing, forever and ever,
where the farm boys sleep with their horses,
and horses hidden in thickets
while the cavalry passes on horses,
and horses pressed against boulders
while the posse passes on horses,
and horses stilled in the hemlocks
while the murderers spur at their horses,
and the hunters go by on their horses
past rivers and castles and mountains.

And still the corporal is rearing upon his stallion in the Louvre,
and the generals sit stiffly astride their bronze studs
in all the public squares of Europe,
and Xanthus sulks with Achilles,
and Pegasus rides from the sea foam,
Al Borak carries Mohammed,
Bucephalus, Alexander,
and Sleipnir trots with Odin
out of the fjords to the ocean;
then out of the long processional friezes
where the marble horses twist and prance for the proud cities
Apollo rides straight up like thunder into the skies.

And the horses rear in the passes
with the horn of Roland winding
and Charlemagne riding his horses
And Joan of Arc at the crossroads
and the highwaymen riding their horses.

Brazillian horses are running,
and the listener sits in the moonlight.
alone on his horse in the moonlight.
Eohippus sleeps in the lavas,
and the Hittites' horses are running;
mesohippus sleeps in the lavas;
the Persian horses are running.
In the steppes the horses are plunging,
with stars just under their forelocks;
they are galloping over the tundra;
they are leaping from mountain to mountain
with hooves aglow in the moonlight.
They have harnessed the waves of the ocean.
They are riding up over our beaches.
They are running wild in our cities.
I love you! I love you!

And then the brown horse and the black horse and the white
    horse
leaped so high in the moonlight that when they came back
    down there was only a dappled one,
and he floated up out of the back pastures over the hills of
    northeastern Iowa.
And when he came to your garden
where you sat in a blue dress on a pallet on the lawn,
his hooves rang like polished bells,
and he knelt on his silken hocks and knees by your side,
laid his slender head gently upon your lap,
looked up at your face with his marble eye,
then folded the silver membrane of his eyelid down,
and slept,
scarcely hearing the apocalypse
galloping away in the shadows.

Joseph Langland

67

COCKTAILS AGAIN

Once more we sit here in this Tavern's court
that used to be a speakeasy in the days
when Prohibition made of pubs a sport
outside the law. That far-back era plays
a phantom role in this, our get-together
in a year that telescopes the fervent past.
We're a different pair, in a different kind of weather,
at a rendezvous we've managed to keep at last.

This ailanthus tree—it was just a struggling sapling,
and surrounding walls had no lichen on weathered stone.
But look how the twilight's luminous roseate dappling
filters about us, again makes the place our own.
Iris still grows; and of this table, mark
how rain has warped it, leaving its rough wood sere
with splinters on its once so smooth and dark
surface. One little leaf's imprisoned here,
preserved, perhaps, forever.

                                                    Ah, my friend,
your eyes are sad. I know. It was last year,
last eon, maybe. What's it in the end
whether we sat here in our age or youth?
Memory? Yes, all retrospect is tinged
with some inexorable moment's flaming truth;
but the great epic sweep of life—is it not hinged
on these same moments? Shall we protest their dying
which opened up the Gate, albeit with pain?
(I can hear the echo of my old blood's crying.)
We are older now. We are having drinks again.

I read your thoughts. The girl you knew is dead
suddenly. You have met me. We are estranged
by the hovering phantoms of lovers. My head
tosses with no careless abandon. I am changed.

And you, my friend? I held your picture too,
straight and sure, clear-eyed. My heart mourns
in this moment, the other days we knew
of belief in Happiness and Unicorns.
I ask nothing now but sweet fables
sometimes to amuse my troubled brain;
sea waves, sunlight, ivy-covered gables,
the apocalyptic message of the rain.
My friend, I have killed windmills, I have shattered
the irrelevant ghosts which once loomed straight and tall
casting their shadows; I have long since battered
to dust a hoax, a high impregnable wall.

Disenchanted? No, I am merely calm
like the veteran of won or failured wars
who holds an insect in his calloused palm
and watches it traverse his sundry scars,
as small or great as was the enemy.

What have I then? Joy, but no joys, my friend;
and Sorrow but no sorrows. Ripeness brings
a clear untained vision of Life's end;
I demand nothing for myself outside
those miracles I took for granted, turned
aside from fretfully: crisp leaves that died
and spread a brittle carpet; suns that burned
at dusk time; the cool creek and massive stone
where I once walked, unseeing. Those remain
ageless and wise with comfort.
                                        I am alone,
my friend, though we have drinks again.

Gladys Merrifield

THE AUTHOR TO HIS BODY
ON THEIR FIFTEENTH BIRTHDAY, 29 ii 80

"There's never a dull moment in the human body."
— *The Insight Lady*

Dear old equivocal and closest friend,
Grand Vizier to a weak bewildered king,
Now we approach The Ecclesiastean Age
Where the heart is like to go off inside your chest
Like a party favor, or the brain blow a fuse
And the comic-book light-bulb of Idea black out
Forever, the idiot balloon of speech
Go blank, and we shall know, if it be knowing,
The world as it was before language once again;

Mighty Fortress, maybe already mined
And readying to blow up grievances
About the lifetime of your servitude,
The body of this death one talkative saint
Wanted to be delivered of (not yet!),
Aggressively asserting your ancient right
To our humiliation by the bowel
Or the rough justice of the elderly lecher's
Retiring from this incontinence to that;

Dark horse, it's you we've put the money on
Regardless, the parody and satire and
The nevertheless forgiveness of the soul
Or mind, self, spirit, will or whatever else
The ever-unknowable unknown is calling itself
This time around—shall we renew our vows?
How should we know by now how we might do
Divorced? Homely animal, in sickness and health,
For the duration; buddy, you know the drill.

Howard Nemerov

MY MOTHER, 87, LIVES

My mother, 87, lives
in San Diego. She moves
from hotel to hotel
because the room is cold
or the food is bad
or they steal her Social Security
checks or they wait in the hall
to mug her.
She moves back and forth
between 2 hotels
and can't recall which one
she lives in.
"She spills things from her purse
then puts it all back again
forgetting what she looked for.
She don't know your address no more."
The manager tells me this
long distance.
I can do nothing
but send my love.

Harold Norse

SKELETON CORAL

My son brings coral
from Bali old beads
he graded and strung
not knowing they entangle me
in an image of dovegray
crepe-de-chine
and a coral frame
for my mother's peachskin face
her amber eyes
dark pompadour,
straightbacked
silent after cooking, washing,
bedding of children are done,
adding the piecework-tags—
the sum
of her day at the factory
sewing machine.

Kaela Petrov-Reynolds

UP IN SMOKE

tobacco to
bac oh go
back oh
go back to
the incense go
back to
the fragrance
the innocence
eye in the
whorled smokey
dream to go back to
the juice
and the bite oh
the time I am
in oh the
sift of the ash
to go back to

Kaela Petrov-Reynolds

NIGHT CHANGES

      furnace
kicks on
in the lightless room
fan bellows-presses
decompresses air
          I am
a single gill
strain, slow, lift, fall
in the thickening
          my dream
is drowning
in high canyon wind
dry oak snakes
against the wall
snags me awake
my eyes are hot
          the fog
seeping in at the window
is a cold
poultice

Kaela Petrov-Reynolds

A PURLEY BLACK STONE

sign say
we be close
all day
we done shut down

doan leave no laun-de-ree
no shirts from the hath-a-way
no sheets from the kay-kay-kay
and doan leave no messed-up towels from the turk

bee-cause
he dead
our mis-ter ed
our pore mis-ter ed
is dead

we gonna hold
a pass-the-hat burr-i-al
at quarter to four
in the back
of the laun-de-ree store
so we kin
buy a stone
for one of our own
a purely black stone
for he grave

bee-cause
he dead
our mis-ter ed
our pore mis-ter ed
is dead

Ann Petry

75

A REAL BOSS BLACK CAT

I keep seen
a black cat
a real boss black cat
who kin fly

He float around
in the air
high up

He swim around
in the air
high up

He go
light and easy
and fast

A real boss black cat

Him I wish
I was

Ann Petry

MEDIATION: MELANCHOLY

bachelor of music,
                    cum laude,
my shadowy lutenist
                    plucking
nightshade;
            my double
(with the pulse
            of a quiet man)
in residence
            on the left
side of my soul,
                    with whom the right side rests
like two pans of a scale
                    at O;
who radiates
            undiminishing in an own phoenix;
have you not put me,
                    my sweet drone,
my genius,
            in touch with Abraham
of my long line?

To borrow the words
                    of Isaak Walton
when he wrote
                    of the nightingale,
"Lord, what music hast thou
provided for the saints in heaven!"

Carl Rakosi

MEDITATION

Psychologist,
                my mental spider,
hero of time,
                what do you make of this?
"Six days sailing
                north of Britain,"
wrote the unknown
                sailor
circa 150 A.D.
                "lies the Utmost Island
of the Sullen Sea."

In such a sea,
                solus,
I lay at zero,
                plumb,
with no way back
                . . . .the dream
had not quite passed
                (like an
early Greek hero,
                I thought, of obscure origin.
There was still
                an instant
image from it
                of deserted streets
and dust and paper
                flying around,
by which I knew
                that the end was approaching

though no way out
                appeared yet from
that turbulent night
                of continual alarums
in which the human race
                came out of the ocean
in frightful import,
                that Passion
staggering to imagine
                in its ordeal,
and passed through time
                before my eyes,
I swear it,
                I meanwhile unreal
as in a fever.

No sooner thought
                then it was image
and like a great wave
                broke
and lapped at the shore.

After which these words
                from the stern,
underlying order
                of things
were spoken
                in my head,
not loud
                but with a heavy
stress
                in the mouth,
exact and absolute
                as a stone engraving:
"Pursuant to the Rocks,
                Thorns!"

I could make nothing
                    of this but poetry
but the utterance was darker
                    and impregnable,
not to be looked at closely
                    nor transcribed
by a stylus on the scale
                    of a lens in
a butterfly's eye.
                    It was meant
to guide me,
          of that I was sure.

That is how I came
                    to know
how God spoke with Moses.

                    Carl Rakosi

MEDITATION

The old man
                drew the line
for his son,
              the executive:
"I don't want you spending money on me!
(not as long as there are fathers)",
the line ageless
                as the independence of time.
Musters tears
              and overflows
the inner ear,
             yet does not matter.
It can not cure frailty.

I seek him
            who will seek me out
and will believe
               what I do not believe
(that is my frailty).
                "Sit down here with us,"
he says,
           "You don't have to impress anyone.
Here is my hand.
             Your age is of no significance."
Ah!
        I move closer to his mouth
and look into his eyes.
                I do not avert mine,
there is no reason to,
             or retreat
into kindly smile.

Ah, companero,
            you were born
on the wrong day
             when God was paradoxical.
You'll have to
          find yourself an old dog.

Carl Rakosi

MEDITATION

Lord, what is man?
He looks into a glass
and sees a physical figure
looking back at him,
the two waiting immobile
for him to reappear
as the world knows him
by name, by work, by habits,
in what particulars
he is significant,
and...why should it be embarrassing
to speak to this?
...in what endearing...
Is he honest?
and how he looks
when meditating...
all in a semblance characteristic
as his bones,
including that shade
in the inwit of presence,
his secondary at the subliminal portal,
that stands for more
potentiality than appears,

the quiet continent
                    behind it feeling boundless
(the worse for him).

The final scene, the only scene,
                           inherent in glass,
is that looker
                waiting for it to happen
and caught in the act.

Carl Rakosi

MEDITATION

What is the nature
            of quintessence?
Since there is no answer,
              the question
must be poetical.
            Yet when Aristotle writes,
"A spirit
         in the body of the seed
whose nature answereth
             in proportion
to the element of the stars,"
              I could touch that
with a fingertip
         and be content.

Can wit sigh,
          "Ah, how lovely that is!"?
(that was my inbreath,
            not my logic)
and have a tear
         in its eye for it?

Out of the way,
         wit!
I am within a breath
          of affinity
and yearn
        for long distances.

Come out, my lamb,
         my mystery.
This spirit
        you can trust.

Carl Rakosi

WONDER

If you were an Arm with an Eye
and a Nose, you'd (objective, fresh-viewing)
soon know how strange we are.

Here for what reason? Who brought us,
Arm? It's weird. I mean brought
all of us, moss-green cockatoos, silk-

screen junkoes, beavers and eager
snakes, sniffing, hugging the
ground like brokers on the traces

of a runaway ticker?   And then
mosquitoes, for the love of God, Arm!
Scorpions, swift as rats, rabbits screaming

like murdered babies and jumping-jack
sun, up-down. Why these, Arm? Smell how strange,
Arm; love's church a hole between excrements.

And worse; Beauty! Why this, why *this*, Arm?
Fields on fields of silver bells pure as
stopped sunlight and then the blinding yellow

flowers, hammered petal-thin right in the
fields by smiths of gold, in worship, yet.
And if you were not an Arm with an Eye

and a Nose but were a Hand with an Ear, you'd
hear   how strange the bees, Hand, like hungry
violins playing up a storm over the drowning

orchard and meaning every note and every pause;
meaning drum of hunger, hum of work, horn of mystery,
strings of love, throat of war, horn of silence.

And if, Hand, you heard a single nightingale
in Greece or England, say, and having no eyes to weep
with, then, perhaps, you might really hear

(caught in this Beauty like quicksand, like
children in amber, beached listening angels)
how utterly strange we are, how weird, Hand.

Leonard Wallace Robinson

THE GIFT

"i never promised you a rowboat."
my father actually said that line
three decades ago; he said it on

my tenth birthday when i cried and
sulked thinking he *had* promised me one.
god alone knows how i came by such an

idea   pure wish   pa simply didn't
believe in such big gifts   none of us
even had a bike though we were far

from poor   eleven kids   and so   i stole
the rowboats of the lobster men as they
lay sleeping in the long hot marshfield

massachusetts afternoons of summer, dreaming
of lobster pots as packed as full
as boiled red lobster claws.   i liked

John Greenleaf's boat the best, oars
always in it, lightest   out our channel
on the ebb i'd shoot into the calm of

cape cod bay   what things i saw   a silver
horse in ten clear yards of water   the
great rust freckles on a sunken checker

taxi   fins were everywhere   wise
dolphins circled me and shining baked clay
starfish danced a glazed descending measure

all was weaving waving formal pattern designed
at the antipodes where winds blew ribs
and ripples in shell and sand in

endless art   provincetown beckoned   it
looked so near i'd want to try it every time
once i did   twenty miles away   it was dark

before i turned back and dark as hell when i
came up the channel   Mr. Greenleaf
was waiting on the muddy shore with folded

arms his rubber boots colossal   but what he
said was "steal it a little earlier after this,
if you don't mind, leonard   i go out at dark."

Leonard Wallace Robinson

CURATOR'S SON AND POET AT THE PIRAEUS

he took me through the naked-kouroi room
where all the lovely boys stood straight and stiff
like soldiers of a pharaoh   their eyes
forever stricken with infinity.

he pointed out the awesome beauty of
their genitals, nates and their hips,
subjects i had never concentrated
on before;   i'd just passed twelve.

much to note, he said;   the scrotal wrinkles,
for examples, contrasting with the textured
grain of thigh as smooth as honey looks;
and prepuces were all-important too,

possessed the power to show the inner
boy as graced or graceless, if, that is, beauty
really did reflect our depths; standards
here are new, he said;   your father would agree.

at twelve that night he took me to
the oddest place i'd seen to meet
a fisherman i'd really like, he said;   a cafe
at piraeus jammed with drunken sailors;

one laughed at him and poked his great
round belly and he giggled foolishly;
but when his friend did not appear
by one, he fell as silent as a stone

his sunken eyes like beryl under sea,
and seemed to me beside him in that din
beside the dark aegean, nakeder and
lovelier than a kouros for his grief.

Leonard Wallace Robinson

ANGER, LONG-TEMPERED, YEARS LATER

How I ran for Grindle on that icy
indoor-outdoor wooden track in Maine;
he had those stopwatch eyes and click-on smile
that said: 'I love him'   'all heart'   he never quits'.

I won Exeter and I won Andover and I won Choate for him
and tied the Lower Maine record for the mile
against Tufts Freshmen. Grindle's click-on
smile turned permanent. I danced from cloud to

peak to cloud and bulldog linesmen on
the football team gave me their quick front
teeth and flag of hand. But then one weekend
down at Stowe, Vermont, I got on skis, though

Grindle had said and more than once, "No
skiing and no skating and don't forget that.
Don't forget." But I forgot or something. I smashed
my knee and never ran again. Flexion gone, a

cut-through cartilage. Oh, I tried. I was absurd,
could only gallop now. He watched me trying but
only from a distance. He never spoke to me again,
never wrote a note saying 'I told you so' or 'We could've

beat in the Olympics, you ass-hole, you featherbrain
pile of galloping horsemeat.' Rage, Anything. I needed help.
Afterward for years I ran for you smoothly like fleeing light,
oh, Grindle, like insane hope oh Timer whose eyes

loved my thunder on the frozen wood but whose silly
ticking mind could not, speed dead, pray for my endurance
                                        to survive.

Leonard Wallace Robinson

SQUALOR AND EARLY SORROW

I was sitting in a kerosene-stove-heated bar
in Hoboken with my girl who loved squalor and
the ex-mayor asked me to put him up in a flop-house
for the night, and later, because I couldn't afford
that he asked me for just another drink and told me
he had learned (in Greece) exactly how
to control the Jersey mosquito who made life
such a terrible misery in that state but I couldn't
pry the secret out of him for three more drinks
on me but when he was ready and willing to talk
he couldn't; she and I went home on the 2 A.M.
ferry and sang so beautifully together on the bow
you'd swear that only love could make such harmony,
but no, she really loved squalor not me who could
only locate it for her and she went off soon after
with a guy she said was a labor leader and I learned
he beat her nearly to death three times when drunk
before she left him for good. Good? Did I say for Good?
Not for her I'll bet. Never. Nice and beautiful as she was.

Leonard Wallace Robinson

WHOLE SALER

i been in vanilla beans this week
up to my ears and in moist-mocha
recently up to the eyes; bought three
chockful gloriettas of steaming

cabooch and mucho corny chowder ingreds,
with small bear-beans, black-eyed boomquats,
some winterwipple and musical pears. i
deal in futures only; martha likes them.

i deal in snow-sugar, web-sugar, darning-
needle brownsalt and i bought two doz.
redrockcandy jetties and a gross of licorice
wirelesses off hatteras for rich nine-year-

olds; *semper paratus*, martha always says; hectare
seedcake soaked in three cloy of hymettus honey and
transportation for it, 30 wagons w/beer-colored
horses, what's to worry, i can always use them,

martha says. grapes are a glut so i
buy a glut all-concord. yes, indeed, the vanilla
beans were winged, soared, i made a killing,
so next week will surely go to sugartree,

molasses-mull, cinnamon-pull and chimney cream
sweets; martha was poor and likes them best.

Leonard Wallace Robinson

IN THE WHALE

In my turqoise sweater, disgruntled
that I was so late, I left my house
in Mexico this morning and stepped
into a crystal light and was caught
like a blue plum in bright sugar-
water, caught in open sunlight, but
down the street under the shade of
that great tree by the underground
water, the river that feeds our town,
was a boy much further along toward
total saturation than me; he was in
a sharp brown-green condition, the
razor light limning him (God alone
knows how through all that shade)
still as a stone against the cheviot
wall, his back and right foot up,
supporting him, his peaked cap in
that actinic rain drenched in mottled
clarities. And just behind him in
full sun, like me, a Mexican woman in
a blue *rebozo* and a basket of tomatoes
on her head, overfull, plunges down
the hilly path full tilt right into
the shade and turns into slow-motion
damsun-blue with light coming through
and strawberry top, and then a white
dog is sucked into the emulsion, gives
up, lies down, and now I, electrified,
magnetic, am drawn over into the jellied
shade, plunge in, and sun surrounds and
shade engulfs all four and now we hang
all motionless together in this morning
miracle, leviathan, force field of grace.

Leonard Wallace Robinson

ARE YOU JUST BACK FOR A VISIT OR
ARE YOU GOING TO STAY?

How the place has grown. I harldy recognize it.
There is new construction everywhere. I had to look for
    the old landmarks.
A lot of the young people seem to be staying, at least
    for a while.
Everybody is building his own house, or is trying to,
The way he wants it or thinks he might be comfortable in.

The old zoning ordinances and building codes have all been
    allowed to lapse,
Which on the whole seems to be a good thing,
Although I suppose there is as much shoddy work in this
    new sprawl
As there ever was in all those old rows and boxes.

The rest of the state never did pay much attention to the
    town,
And still doesn't,
Which really never mattered:
To be well remembered in the town was all any sensible
    townsman ever wanted.

When I left
Everybody knew everybody else, or seemed to,
At least their names and where they lived.
Doc Williams and the lawyer in the insurance business
    had the best houses in town.

Most of the really old houses had been pulled down
    before I left.
I was surprised to see two or three have been refurbished
And seem highly regarded.
But no one seems to know anyone else now
Although you can't really tell unless you live there.
Perhaps I should have stayed.

There is a lot of new building to the west.
On the south side there is a whole area of impressive new
    town houses
Although as you drive by all the exteriors look pretty
    much alike.
There were always a visiting Britisher or two
And some townspeople who thought they were
And I suppose there still are. You can't tell anymore
    from the architecture.

It was hard to make a living there
And I suppose it still is except maybe out by the college.
Win had a rich wife which helped and made it worse.
Miss Spencer who was black stayed mostly in her garden.
A lot of us tried it for a while and then moved away.
Among those who stayed the suicide rate was pretty high.

I recognize a lot of the old houses.
Somehow I thought I might hear a familiar voice say:
Hey, are you just back for a visit or are you going to
    stay?

Francis Coleman Rosenberger

OLD HOMESTEAD REVISITED

No ghosts haunt the screen of manicured hedges
nor glide the weedless sheen of the grass.
Young Puck in the foliage, old witches in thickets
have fled the slick pruning of possible windfalls.

All shadows are neat.

The chimneys and porticoes thoroughly scoured
of clematis and ivy, the eaves guttered straight,
the shaggy old clapboards smoothed in aluminum,
the porch steps carpentered solid and safe.

The door does not creak.

Does doormat spell, "Apparitions not welcome?"
In hallway the wall-to-wall plushness of carpet
would smother a footfall weird on the stairway
and wraiths be dispelled in machine-tempered air.

Hello—o—o. Is anyone there?

No chair left still rocking, no spectacles lying
upon open page, and no kicked-off slippers
or half-empty cup. On the rosewood sofa
new-tufted in satin, no rumpled afghan.

Do humbly beg pardon.

Dorothy Russell

A WOMAN FROM MEMPHIS

O Woman from Memphis, I will try to put down
For all deprived, unfortunate, unaware souls
To pick up on, the mode of your recent operations,
Your style in your newly-conquered domain.

                                                First,
At breakfast: coffee, the Washington Post, with sage
Speculation at headlines and Buchwald. Then, audaciously
Hatted, long-legged in elegant slacks, you sally
Forth, and descend on the clerks in the shops in your
        swirling
And colorful glad arrival. Orders, chit-chat,
Chidings and cries: like birds in the flutter of gathering.
Returning with loads and confusion, a push-cart, mail,
Laundry, delivery boys, you burst in to show
High displeasure at grayness. Turn on the lights!
Radio music to go with your household campaigns!
War on kitchen disorder! Strife on the terrace!
Onslaughts on rugs! Assaults on all unmade beds!
Having conquered, sipping a coke, you gleefully brag
Of your recent triumphs. And certainly it is true,
Miss Consonant Dropper from Way Back, those soft sounds
Of your outlandish tongue invoke a spell on policemen,
Clerks and workmen. Sensing your droll and fierce
Mock-serious queenliness, they can only surrender.
You accept their fealty. Honor for all. Forward!

Immersement in games. Tongue-chewing concentration
At bridge and acrostic. Raptness for hesitant putts.

And growing things! How they engage your marveling
Attention! Green and colorful plants surround you-
Haggled over, lugged, earthed in a rich profusion,
Troweled and tended. Small weak things to encourage
In their coming forth, to rejoice in their young upshooting
And budding accomplishment. Come here, come look, see!
And your warm indrawn breath-catchments for fallers and toddlers
Learners and triers, and all outreachers! Your service
Will never lack for enlistments! Your partisans are children,
Old women, cripples, the sick, and the victims of the times.

The observer of all these wonders, your husband, late comer
To these surprises, amazed always at the twisty,
Unforeseen sallies, saltiness from the boudoir,
Badinage of the bed, and the unexpected kind acts,
Is overcome. How in the world can it be,
This very agreeable state of affairs? He sees
Your proud and fitting sway on your newest stage,
How you deck it with an elaboration of small
And charming things: flowers, figurines, pictures
And sculpture, dolls, picked to enhance the setting
Of your chosen role. He hopes, woman from Memphis,
For you and for him, for the marriage, a reasonable time.

Robert Sargeant

OUR STORY

Remind me again—together we
trace our strange journey, find
each other, come on laughing.
Some time we'll cross where life
ends. We'll both look back
as far as forever, that first day.
I'll touch you—a new world then.
Stars will move a different way.
We'll both end. We'll both begin.

Remind me again.

William Stafford

A STORY THAT COULD BE TRUE

If you were exchanged in the cradle and
your real mother died
without ever telling the story
then no one knows your name,
and somewhere in the world
your father is lost and needs you
but you are far away.

He can never find
how true you are, how ready.
When the great wind comes
and the robberies of the rain
you stand on the corner shivering.
The people who go by—
you wonder at their calm.

They miss the whisper that runs
any day in your mind,
"Who are you really, wanderer?"—
and the answer you have to give
no matter how dark and cold
the world around you is:
"Maybe I'm a king."

William Stafford

ANOTHER OLD GUITAR

For years I was tuned a few notes too high—
I don't see how I could stand it!
You can imagine the strain, hours of
'teen parties, and then beach trips with
"Michael rowed the boat. . ." and later
the marches in all weather singing "We
shall overcome. . . ." Then I moved on.

Now I play in an Eskimo band in Alaska.
I'll never get back outside, through storms;
I dream of returning under a river, breathing
through a straw, carried where the current
hides itself by being just the river. . . .
No. We play in the tin buildings
for the Air Force, and always end with
a relaxed little number the band call
their national anthem: "Somebody, Maybe."

William Stafford

101

ASK ME

Some time when the river is ice ask me
mistakes I have made. Ask me whether
what I have done is my life. Others
have come in their slow way into
my thought, and some have tried to help
or to hurt: ask me what difference
their strongest love or hate has made.

I will listen to what you say.
You and I can turn and look
at the silent river and wait. We know
the current is there, hidden; and there
are comings and goings from miles away
that hold the stillness exactly before us.
What the river says, that is what I say.

William Stafford

SITTING UP LATE

Beyond silence, on the other side merging
deep in the night, a wolf call lifted slowly
teasing farther than air extended,
thrilling into one pinpoint
across the ice.

The rest of my life
there never comes a simple feeling,
or warmth, or success, for always mingled
in the world is what I knew then
crystalized into a dark faith,
absolute,
between one breath and the next.

William Stafford

WHISPERED INTO THE GROUND

Where the wind ended and we came down
it was all grass. Some of us found
a way to the dirt—easy and rich.
When it rained, we grew, except
those of us caught up in leaves, not touching
earth, which always starts things.
Often we sent off our own
just as we'd done, floating that
wonderful wind that promised new land.

Here now spread low, flat on this
precious part of the world, we miss
those dreams and the strange old places
we left behind. We quietly wait.
The wind keeps telling us something
we want to pass on to the world:
Even far things are real.

William Stafford

ABSENCES

Once when the waves were talking one said
"I'll never be back." And then the rest
ran on toward shore, but that one went forth
so far it's never been seen again.

When you walk along sometimes, you think
of that absent wave—and of all that doesn't
exist any more, things of the other
years. "They'll never be back," you say.

You stop and look out, It's already tomorrow
somewhere, and someone like you is walking;
a wave is beginning to speak, and the rest
shrug and go on. You stand and care.

Much has never existed, you know.
You think of things to say. The waves
come in. Wherever you walk you see
a place for that wave. But it isn't there.

William Stafford

GLIMPSES

One time when the wind blows it is years
from now. I am talking with others and
we are telling all the stories except
the one we are in, then someone starts ours:
the wind stops, we look back and then forward.
The voice carries us on and we try to be what it says.

There is an embrace on a street corner;
two people greet and make obsolete all the past.
They research those years for the key
event that separated them, but they can't
find it. They part again, and they never
find what it is they have missed.

Walking along, any time,
I find clues to tomorrow—how hard
a poppy is orange, how alert the leaves
are where the streetlight finds them.
My debt to the world begins again,
that I am part of this permanent dream.

At someone's pretensions a thought comes—Saint Augustine:
a morning cloud throws a shadow but the sun
says light. Our time goes on, a spider
spins, the wind examines the ground
for clues—just being is a big enough job,
no time for anything else.

William Stafford

WAITING IN LINE

You the very old, I have come
to the edge of your country and looked across,
how your eyes warily look into mine
when we pass, how you hesitate when
we approach a door. Sometimes
I understand how steep your hills
are, and your way of seeing the madness
around you, the careless waste of the calendar,
the rush of people on buses. I have
studied how you carry packages,
balancing them better, giving them attention.
I have glimpsed from within the gray-eyed look
at those who push, and occasionally even I
can achieve your beautiful bleak perspective
on the loud, inattentive, shoving boors
jostling past you toward their doom.

With you, from the pavement I have watched
the nation of the young, like jungle birds
that scream as they pass, or gyrate on playgrounds,
their frenzied bodies jittering with the disease
of youth. Knowledge can cure them. But
not all at once. It will take time.

There have been evenings when the light
has turned everything silver, and like you
I have stopped at a corner and suddenly
staggered with the grace of it all: to have
inherited all this, or even the bereavement
of it and finally being cheated!—the chance
to stand on a corner and tell it goodby!
Every day, every evening, every
abject step or stumble, has become heroic:—

You others, we the very old have a country.
A passport costs everything there is.

William Stafford

REMEMBERING

When there was air, when you could
breathe any day if you liked, and if you
wanted to you could run, I used to
climb those hills back of town and
follow a gully so my eyes were at ground
level and could look out through grass as the stems
bent in their tensile way, and see snow
mountains follow along, the way distance goes.

Now I carry those days in a tiny box
wherever I go. I open the lid like this
and let the light glimpse and then glance away.
There is a sigh like my breath when I do this.
Some days I do this again and again.

William Stafford

LURES
(For Charley)

It was timber-raped land
in that high north,
the stumps of white pine left
like riddled tombs
in the midst of slash
and upstart, peasant jacks.
But in winter, long after
the mosquitoes' narrow whine,
our lakes were fat with ice
and food-keen pike.

        We hunted them
in their cold palaces.
We is a braggart's term.
I was a child but I helped
when my grandfather
with heavy thumbs
and pipe-grooved lip
make his crude lures from whittled scrap.
They seemed to me high art,
those rigid minnow shapes
let down through green-blue circles
sawed in a fishhouse floor
to tempt the hungry gleams beneath.

Our rude bait swiveled, swam,
at the set line's end,
adorned with hooks.
They flashed like dreams of jewels
though they were dreamless fakes,
their fins and tails cut from a coffee tin.
A hunk of solder in the belly
weighed them down.
Mine was the final touch:
the burning-in with a redhot pick
of eyes and gills,
even an upturned mouth.
I was good at this, people said,
and I took pride.

                        I wonder now
how much my smiling decoys helped
to kill.

                What I remember—
and without guilt—
is the sweet flesh steaming on my plate,
and how the old man and I,
in silence, bowed over it,
and ate. . .and ate.

                        Adrien Stoutenburg

FACT VERSUS FANCY, & VICE VERSA

Fact is anybody's toy:
yours, mine, the government's.
It goes around naked,
a thing of many bones
without song or any of the fancies
of snow walking in a white cape
or rain going on slender gray canes.

Fact is neither brute nor angel.
It is a ball to be juggled
by any acrobat or clown.
If it has any wings at all
they resemble the tissue arms
of a stick-model plane
built from balsa and rubber
and a cement that makes a household smell
like varnished bananas.
The propellor must be turned
with a dreaming forefinger,
though even then things snap
and fact grinds, nose to the ground,
the wheels turned
into still, dead decimals.

Adrien Stoutenburg

DEATH OF THE BIGTOP

We always feared the earth
might fall, some fault
unhinging all the strings and knots
that hold the work in place. . . .
but that the sky should sag
like the patched roof
of an enormous, wounded tent!

Not swiftly yet;
more a descending chill,
the center pole,
half-visible through clotted air,
beginning to sway.

The highwire shrills
and something, someone, falls;
the ultimate acrobat, some say.

At night the stars skid low
above the Midway strip
to cast an acid glow on frantic clowns,
menagerie, and Wild West show.
They leave a rime like sooty flame
but evidence of fire deceives.
Their torches are almost out, and the sun,
our greatest star, is darker every dawn.
The troposphere's rotting breath will freeze
even our gaudiest spectaculars
of space or muddy hippodrome.

The impresario looks numb.
The hawkers shiver and turn blue.
Some giant thermostat has gone awry,
or else zero was always the sum
our calculated risks led to.

Adrien Stoutenburg

JANUSZ KORCHAK

Guards standing all around
pushing people toward barbed wire:
Deportation Point-Umschlagplatz.
Crowds carry their possessions;
prayer-shawls, phylacteries, books.
The 'haupt-artz' Nahum Remba,
pushes his saintly figure toward
a children formation, marching
with fear in their innocent faces
toward cattle trains;
"Where are they taken us?"—some ask.
It seems awkward to be going on
a picnic in such filthy, smelly wagons.
But, they don't panic, their teacher
and guardian Janusz Korchak walks along.
Weary, sad is his brow, despair, grief
is written on his face, but,
soft and calm is his voice. . .
Remba grabs Korchak's arm, whispers;
"Look dear Janusz, don't try to
be a saint, You know where-to
these tracks are leading, there is
no way you can help your orphans,
we want to take you out of here,
so you can write, survive this war."
"My dear Remba, useless are your words,
if my children are in a grip of death,
I will not deceive them, or leave them,
I doubt if I could carry the burden
of living without these little hands.
No force can keep me away from them,
their fate is my destiny."

Children climb cattle cars, some stumble, cry,
they are pushed into the wagons by the guards.
Janusz Korchak follows them, the cars are shut,
in the darkness dry mouths complain no air,
little hearts beating with horror, weep loudly.
In the midst of the blackness, a familiar voice
asks them to sing the new melody they learned.
Voices of boys and girls spread over the Platz,
the throngs of people are listening in silence,
the SS-henchmen, gendarmes can't believe their ears,
all turn their faces to the moving cattle cars
youthful voices penetrate the air: Ani Maamin,
Ani Maamin Be'emunah Sheley'ma. . .Ani Maa'aamin!

Herman Taube

WINTER MOON

Frozen weeds, frost on the windshield, house of the dead
      closed down for the winter;
by the roadside a crabapple broken into tears brittle
      as ice splintering wheels
cold steel in the sky, you freeze my soul
Three quarters ago you were a dagger at my breast
I shed red blood for your beauty's sake, now
in one of your distant moods you show to a waking world
the thin edge of despair

Joy! Joy! Joy! the crow at noon will sing and the
      gray hawk answer Joy! Joy! Joy!

Once, before men trampled you, you came to me, silver queen,
dancing dress shimmering, diamonds, touch tender as a
      moonbeam
We loved, you and I, fullness for fullness but I was a
      moonchild then
floating in moonlight
and it was June

Obi woman, are you turning on me an evil eye?
Are you writing my obituary in the sky?

Mildred Raynolds Trivers

115

60th BIRTHDAY

Only more sure of all I thought was true. —Frost.
I am blest by everything,
Everything I look upon is blest. —Yeats.

Only less sure of all I never knew.
Always more awed by what is never new.
Computer, spare the mustang's randomness.

There was an oracle. On Samothrace?
There have been tablets. Here? Some greener place?
I (leaf) paint leaves that (falling) try to dance.

Have seen the big death, felt the little death:
The icy and the April breathlessness.
And understand them less and less and less.

Have met the loam-fed and the plastic wreath:
Statesman and hack. Two frightening frightened boys.
Both more endearing than the consequence.

Have heard your rebels and have heard your guild:
And still can't tell the standard from the stance
When both are so rehearsed a cheering noise.

Have squandered silver and have hoarded pence.
Have watched the ant-hill build, burn up, rebuild
(The running is and isn't meaningless)

At Ilium. Or will it be South Bend?
I'll grudge the run a meaning in the end
When wounds that might wound back or else "transcend"

Have risked—instead—to be. Not even bless.

Peter Viereck

116

I HAVE BEEN SPONTANEOUS IN BERMUDA*

Your senile baby-talk with God
Is not with God. "With whom?"
Whom, whom does all amnesia remember?
"No, I'll eacape *her*
By taking to the hills." *Whose hills?*
* * * *

"Before I grew up, rain was a woman calling.
Now that I'm more than man (am now the cosmic
Busybody), why does my 'more' mean less?"
Umbilical to nothing because to all.
"My almost-metal belly asks of metal:
'Are belly-buttons stapled on or soldered?'
I get an answer, but I can't connect it:
'At least there's less malaria, no beggars.' "
Is unearthed earth still earthy?
"Just because my ec-tech threatens her with hysterectomy,
Must buggies and bugs clog progress again?
Rain, rain, go away; no, come back, don't be silent at me;
Forceps slipped, but next time perfect."
Cain always thought he was Abel,
Pre-emptively defending himself.
"I—male, will, steel—pushed ploughs;
Goosed earth; ran-trains-on-time.
I have done the state some service, and I know't."
For example, digital wrist-watches.
"I doubt astrology, I don't doubt vitamin E.
Once I had me a dark night of the soul;
It must have been something I ate.
Brotherhood of the Grail of antiseptic bulldozers,
All you senior citizens with unlined faces,
Pray for my thermostat now and in the hour of ice."
* * * *

*Editors' Note: The two speakers are voices in one
skull. The voice of technic man (this is to tell
them apart) has been printed in quotation marks while that
of timeless man is in italics.

117

Flashback. Back to tribal dawn:
Cave nights, cave lights.
From that first campfire, two rival flames:
A ring, a line.
"*Cave days, stone ways.*
That dawn the choice was male:
Not cycle; flint-tipped will.
Her circle warms the rain;
Her sleep hears leaves unfold.
You chose the second flame;
It jets but cannot heal.
Your jet from chipped flint to—what's the latest? Mars?—
Stays anchored in (gods are gods) Mars.
"We've jetted loose from iron and ax
But haven't."
The more ingenious the metal,
The cruder the hand.
"Did the caveman who genius'd the wheel
Stop painting the wall?"
Caliban wasn't Caliban, Prospero was.
* * * *

"Now, when guffawing in cahoots with wheels,
I boil whole countrysides in eight-lane tar,
What dirty goatfoot stomps graffiti on?"
Dirt blooms. "Will builds. " *Say: will upholsters.*
"Bloom sleeps; will bustles." *Say: bloom is serene*
Explosion. "Will is lively." *Lively*
Is not alive; a funeral pyre
Is snugger than her hearth
A while.
"But ac—ac—our—ackack—ACTIVITY—"
A loyal bustling nuclear reactor's
Leak. "Mek*
Has its own momentum. Matter
Has its heart

*Mek, the Hittite root for power, passed via San-
skrit into our Greek and Latin roots for "machine."

Of which heart knows nothing.
I'm *happy;* super this and super that;
I have been spontaneous in Bermuda."
She won't embarrass you with public pity;
But when dying hurts, she'll be
There, holding your hand.
"All I really wanted was to be loved;
I was ready for any compromise; some won't cooperate;
Secret sympathizers with germs. Is rain's silence
Her reproach to Saharas? I yearn to raise funds for
Fund raisers. Gloves between me and touch."
Lascaux. Chartres. Chunky once.
"Alone in pairs, I fuss with dials. Well,
I'll work and travel; supersonics, yogurt.
I feel so free now, except sometimes."
For a while it was good to have been man.

Peter Viereck

MAINSTAY
(for Hoppy on his twentieth birthday)

I

Hoppy, you crept out
onto the porch, collapsing
on the shag-rug, ragged lump,
meowing absentmindedly
and yet insistently, sleep,
age—and August-drugged,
still burdening—
　　　　　your look
　　like Socrates just after
　　the Symposium or during
　　his trial and the long vigil
　　prompted by the final drug,

　　or like Picasso old
　　his mistress and the maid
　　(was it his wife?) must each
　　day drag out of his bed,

　　but most of all
　　that aged Jew, with his last
　　breath begging, "Please be
　　so kind, a glass tea"—
how much can I expect
of you?
　　　　　More than ever
you suffer my affection
even when it rouses
into gusts of roughhouse.
For you know me well
enough to know it ends
in food and purring hugs.

II

But now, a front tooth
gone, one nicked ear slack,
your leftpaw whiskers bitten
off, you totter
                over images
too swift, too vague—many
a mouse and bird once stalked,
the chipmunks, chattering—
for you to keep.
                Like you
badly tattered, pretty much
used up, all your nine
lives seem sadly huddled
side by side.
                And any dream,
any high-falutin fear,
I might be urging you
to share you disregard,

        like that aged Jew,
        Picasso still on the scent,
        the rest forgot, or Socrates,
        set on the final argument.
Yet here you are, gazing
up at me, with briefly
calculating eyes, gold-
amber still, the appetite
behind—its very gnawing
strength engrossing you—
a help of sorts, mainstay.

                        Theodore Weiss

Biographical Notes

Martha Bartlett lives in Boston, where she is a member of the Porch Poets, a group of women poets of various ages and backgrounds.

Guy R. Beining lives in Jackson Heights, NY. *A New Boundary And Other Pieces*, Woodrose Editions, 1980.

Charles G. Bell teaches at St. John's College, Santa Fe, NM. He is a novelist as well as poet; and since 1939 he has been composing in a slide-tape art form, seeking a reconstitution of poetic tragedy. *The Half Gods*, Ultramarine, 1968.

Etta Blum, Santa Fe, NM, has published translations from the Yiddish of short stories by Eliezer Blum-Alquit and poems by Jacob Glatstein. *The Space My Body Fills*, The Sun Stone Press, second edition, 1981.

Pearl Bond lives in Saugerties, NY. *The Unicorn Love Poems*, 1979.

James Broughton, curently a member of the faculty of the San Francisco Art Institute, is a playwright and avant-garde filmmaker as well as poet. *Hymns to Hermes*, ManRoot, 1979.

LoVerne Brown, former newspaper reporter and poetry magazine editor in Alaska and California, now teaches part-time in the "Coping with Government" program of San Diego State University.

Charles Bukowski, who lives in Los Angeles, has been an editor, columnist, and prolific writer of poetry, fiction, and nonfiction. *Burning in Water, Drowning in Flame*, Black Sparrow, 1980.

Elmira Bussey lived for ninety-one years in the Boston area, where she worked as an illustrator. *Among The Missing*, 1978.

Olga Cabral, a New York poet, of Portuguese descent, has been an office worker, art gallery owner, and director of a children's art workshop. *In The Empire of Ice*, West End Press, 1980.

Eleanor Davidson Calenda lives in New York City. Recently her poems have appeared in *Voices from A Third Age*, *Bitterroot*, and *Wind*.

Lillie D. Chaffin teaches at Eastern Kentucky University, Pikeville. She has published numerous books of poetry, fiction, nonfiction, and pictures. *We Be Warm Till Springtime Comes*, Macmillan, 1980.

Elizabeth Eddy is a Chicago artist (painting, drawing), editor, and poet, whose poems recently have appeared in *Ms.*, *Hollow Spring Review*, *Poetry & Syncline*.

Béla Egyedi, who lives in Montreal, was born and educated in Hungary. He was captured by the Soviet Army near the end of WWII and interned in a forced labor camp, from which he escaped in 1948, to become an artist, linguist, and poet in exile. His poems recently have appeared in *Antigonish Review* and *Poetry/Windsor/Poesie*.

Vesle Fenstermaker lives in Indianapolis. She has published short stories and novels as well as poetry. Recently her poems have appeared in *Kansas Quarterly*, *Spoon River Quarterly*, and *The New York Times*.

Margaret Flanagan, of Saratoga Springs, NY, served in the Women's Army Corps in New Guinea, the Philippines, China, and Panama (Canal Zone). Having recently returned to "an early love, writing," she has seen her poems published in many magazines and has won the Sri Chimnoy Prize for Spiritual Poetry.

Ethel Nestell Fortner has retired to a farm in Estacada, OR, after a career as teacher and school administrator. More than 200 of her poems have appeared in magazines. *Clouds & Keeping*, Cascade Press, 1973.

Robert Francis lives in his famous house, Fort Juniper, in Amherst, MA. *Collected Poems, 1936-1976*, University of Massachusetts Press, 1976.

Robert Friend is a translator of Hebrew poetry and a teacher at Hebrew University, Jerusalem. *Selected Poems*, Seahorse Press, 1976.

James Hearst was born and raised on Maplehearst Farm, Iowa. After farming with his brother until his early forties, he joined the English faculty of Northern Iowa University. *Snake in The Strawberries*, Iowa State University Press, 1979.

Edwin Honig, who teaches at Brown University, Providence, RI, has published many volumes of poetry, plays, criticism, and translations. *Selected Poems*, Texas Center for Writers Press, 1979.

Barbara Howes now lives in North Pownal, VT, after having resided in England, France, Haiti, Italy, and New York City, where she edited *Chimera* magazine. *A Private Signal*, Wesleyan University Press, 1978.

Josephine Jacobsen lives in Baltimore. She has served as Poetry Consultant to the Library of Congress, and, since 1973, as Honorary Consultant in American Letters. *The Chinese Insomniacs*, University of Pennsylvania Press, 1981

Joseph Langland spent the early part of his life mostly in Iowa. Since 1959 he has resided in Amherst, where he taught at The University of Massachusetts. *Any Body's Song*, Doubleday, 1980.

Gladys Merrifield, a Californian by birth and education, currently lives in New York City, where for many years she was editor and staff writer for *Family Circle* magazine. Her poems have appeared in many magazines, including *The Lyric West* and *Poet Lore*.

Howard Nemerov teaches at Washington University, St. Louis. He received the National Book Award and the Pulitzer Prize for his *Collected Poems*, Univeristy of Chicago Press, 1977.

Harold Norse, who currently lives in Monte Rio, CA, has taught writing and literature in California, New York, Europe, and North Africa. He was associated with William S. Burroughs and the Cut-up experimental writing technic in Paris, 1960-63, and edited the literary/arts magazine, *Bastard Angel*, in San Francisco, 1972-75. *Carnivorous Saint: Gay Poems 1941-1976*, Gay Sunshine Press, 1977.

Kaela Petrov-Reynolds lives in Kensington, CA, where she does secretarial work for her living.

Ann Petry, who lives in Old Saybrook, CT, is known for her short stories and for her plays for children.

Carl Rakosi, who lives in San Francisco, earned his way for many years working as a social worker and psychotherapist. He is often thought of in terms of his work as an Objectivist. *My Experiences in Parnassus*, Black Sparrow, 1977.

Leonard Wallace Robinson lives in San Miguel de Allende, Mexico. He is a novelist and short story writer as well as poet, and has worked as reporter, writer, and/or editor for magazines and presses including *The New Yorker*, *Esquire*, *Colliers*, and Holt, Rinehart. Novel: *The Man Who Loved Beauty*, Harper and Row, 1976, and New American Library, 1977.

Francis Coleman Rosenberger lives in McClean, VA. After publishing poems in many magazines during the late 1930s and early 1940s, he took a leave of absence, from which he has recently returned to see his new poems in magazines including *Laurel Review*, *Poetry*, *Arizona Quarterly*, and *Southern Poetry Review*.

Dorothy Russell lives in Chardon, OH. At 82 she has begun submitting poems for publication, with the encouragement of her creative writing professor, Grace Butcher.

Robert Sargeant lives in Arlington, VA. He was brought up in Louisiana and Mississsippi, but has lived since the middle 1940s in the Washington D.C., area. *A Women from Memphis*, The Word Works, 1979.

William Stafford lives in Lake Oswego, OR, but has been identified by teachers and editors with every region in the United States. In 1963 he received the National Book Award for his book of poems, *Traveling Through The Dark. Stories That Could Be True: New and Collected Poems*, Harper and Row, 1977.

Adrien Stoutenburg, who lives in Santa Barbara, CA, has published more than 30 books of fiction and nonfiction for young readers, as well as several books of poetry. *Greenwhich Mean Time*, University of Utah Press, 1979.

Herman Taube was raised in Lodz, Poland, where his family perished during WWII. After surviving a Soviet forced labor camp in Central Asia, he was repatriated, and he then made his way to the United States, where he has made his home in Washington, D.C. He has written his poems mainly in Yiddish, and then translated some of them into English; but recently he has been composing directly in English. *A Chain of Images*, 1975.

Mildred Trivers, born in Ohio, lived in Germany and Switzerland during the years preceding WWII, then in Washington, D.C., while serving as a State Department wife, and then in Copenhagen, Berlin, and Zurich, as a Foreign Service wife. Upon retiring, she and her husband settled in Muncie, IN. *If You Want A Modern Mother*, Barnwood Press, 1981.

Peter Viereck lives in South Hadley, MA. He is an historian and prize-winning translator. His book of poems, *Terror and Decorum*, 1948, won the Pulitzer Prize. Forthcoming: *Applewood*, a collection of new poems.

Theodore Weiss lives in Princeton, NJ, where he teaches at Princeton and edits the *Quarterly Review of Literature. Views and Spectacles*, Macmillan, 1979.